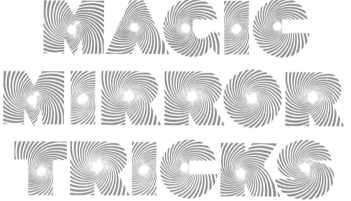

MAGIC MIRROR TRICKS

former title: Another Magic Mirror Book
original hardcover title: Look at Annette

devised **by Marion Walter**
illustrated **by Navah Haber-Schaim**

SCHOLASTIC INC.
New York Toronto London Auckland Sydney

ISBN 0-590-40875-5

16 15 14 13 12 11 10 9   3 4 5/9

To my niece Annette
who likes to pick daisies

Can you see Annette?

Hi, Annette!

Hi there, Mike!

Sometimes they are happy.

But sometimes they are sad.

Who is happy?

Who is sad?

Make Annette look happy.

Now make her look sad!

Annette has one ribbon
in her hair.
Can you put the other one there?
What else can you do?

On his foot Mike has one shoe.

Put the other one on too.

Their pet looks funny.

Is it a cat?

Or is it a bunny?

Can you see

                their red ball?

Can you see it all?

What else can you change?

Annette has a bear.

Put all of him there!

Here is the bear.

What can you do

so that Mike has one too?

They would like to have more.

Can you see three — or four?

Mike likes to watch birds

hop and fly.

Now you can make some more

hop by!

What else can you see?

Annette likes to pick daisies.

Can you see many?

Or hardly any?

They like to hang clothes
out to dry.
Want to help them?
You can try.

Hang more clothes on the line.
When they're dry, take them off.

Now you have met Annette and Mike.

Good-bye, Annette!

So long, Mike!